EXTRAORDINARY MILITARY KIDS

A WORKBOOK FOR AND ABOUT MILITARY KIDS

Written by

Megan Numbers, MA, LPC

Illustrated By

Jax Bennett

HELLGATE PRESS   ASHLAND, OREGON

HELLGATE PRESS
PO Box 3531
Ashland, OR 97520
email: info@hellgatepress.com

Cover & Interior Design: L. Redding
Illustrations: Jax Bennett
Jax Bennett Photo: Abi Sperati

Cataloging In Publication Data available from the publisher by request.
ISBN: 978-1-55571-892-3

Printed and bound in the United States of America
First edition 10 9 8 7 6 5 4 3 2 1

To my extraordinary military kids, LJ and Logan.
I love you infinity times a thousand! —Megan

To my sweet little boy, Gavin, who
makes my life complete. Xoxo —Jax

Hi! I'm Mike!
I'm not an ordinary kid; I'm EXTRA ordinary because I'm a military kid! I'm going to take you on a journey about my military life, and hopefully I'll learn about your life, too! But first, let me introduce you to my friends...

M
ISABELLA
TJ
ANTHONY

Did you know that there are 2 million military kids? That's a lot!
LANDON
IRENE
RORY
DRAW A PORTRAIT OF YOURSELF HERE!
YOU

Being a military kid can be tough at times, but it can also be super cool! Here are some cool dudes and dudettes who were military kids, too!

Jessica Alba

Bruce Willis

Tiger Woods

Shaquille O'Neal

Elton John

Ciara

Martin Lawrence

Kathy Lee Gifford

John McCain

John Kerry

Christina Aguilera

Who are some awesome people you know that are or have been military kids?

1._____________________________________

2._____________________________________

3._____________________________________

Draw a picture of your military friends.

Did you know that military kids are 2x
more likely to join the military
than non-military kids?

When I grow up, I want to be in the Army
just like my mom, dad, grandfather,
and uncle were.

My dad was in the Army, but he's retired now.
My mom is active duty, so we still move around
all over the country. I have a little sister, Isabella,
and a step-brother, David, who lives in Texas.

I miss him a lot, but he comes to visit during the
holidays and over summer break. We also have
a dog, Meadow. We got her when we were
stationed at Fort Carson, CO.

Tell me about your military family!

____

____

____

____

____

____

____

____

____

____

Draw a picture of your family doing something together.

Here are the states and bases where I've lived:

Fort Hood, TX
Schofield Barracks, HI
Fort Carson, CO
Fort Bragg, NC

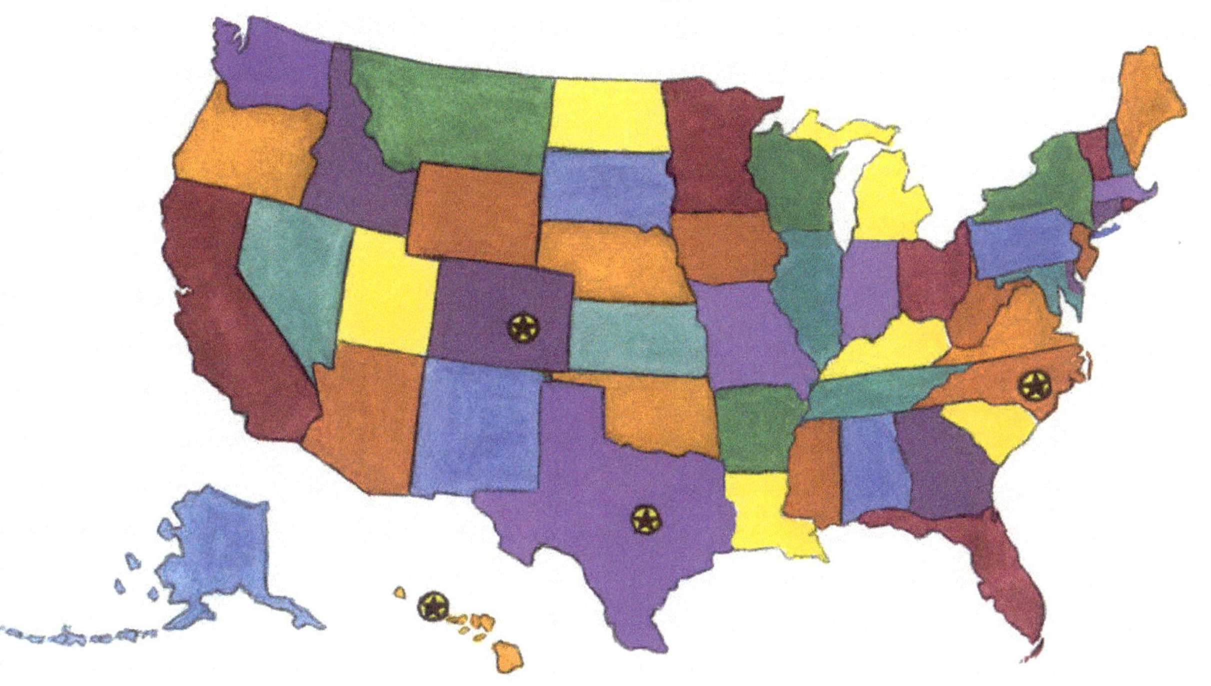

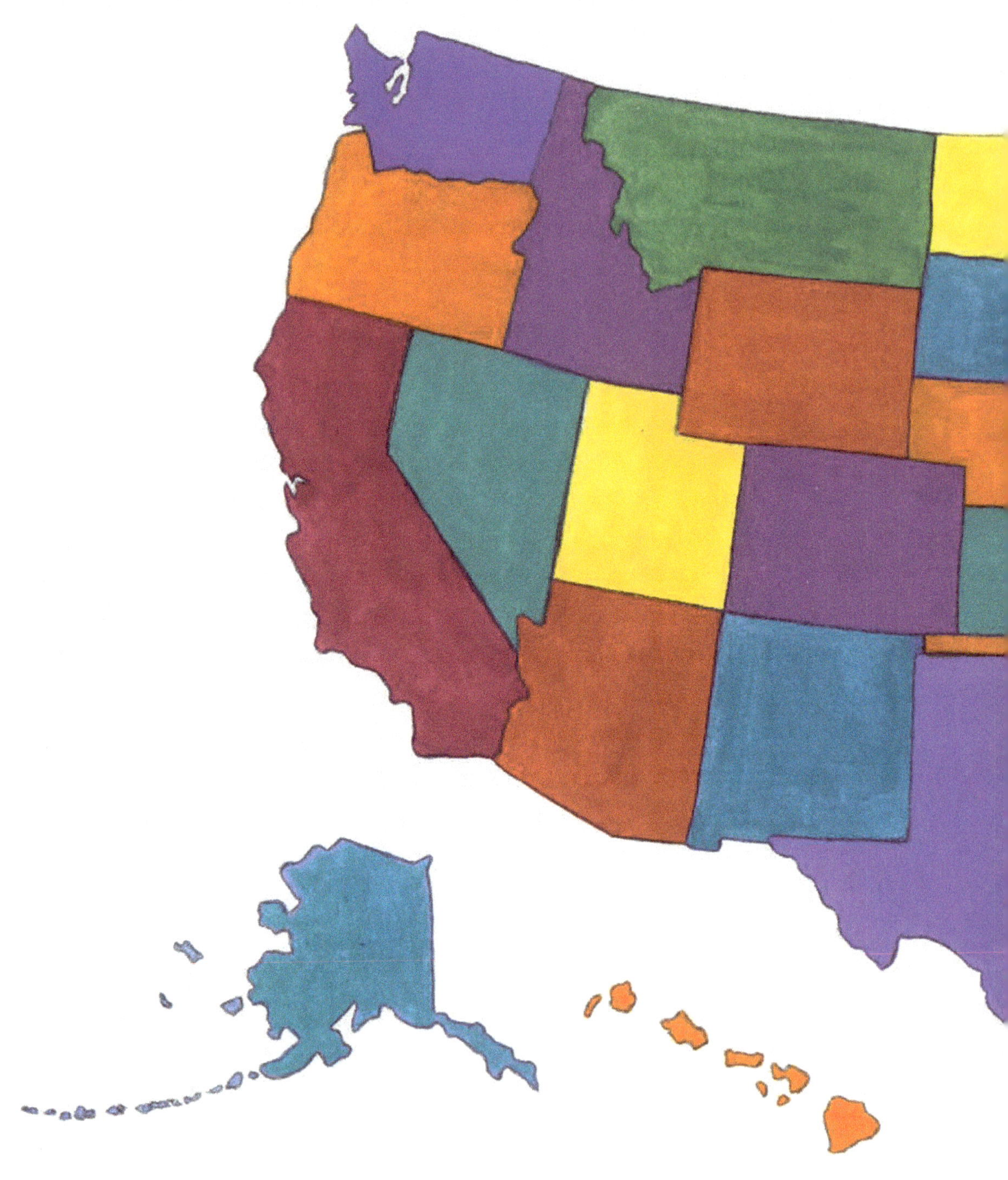

Write down the places and bases where you've
lived or visited and star them on your map:

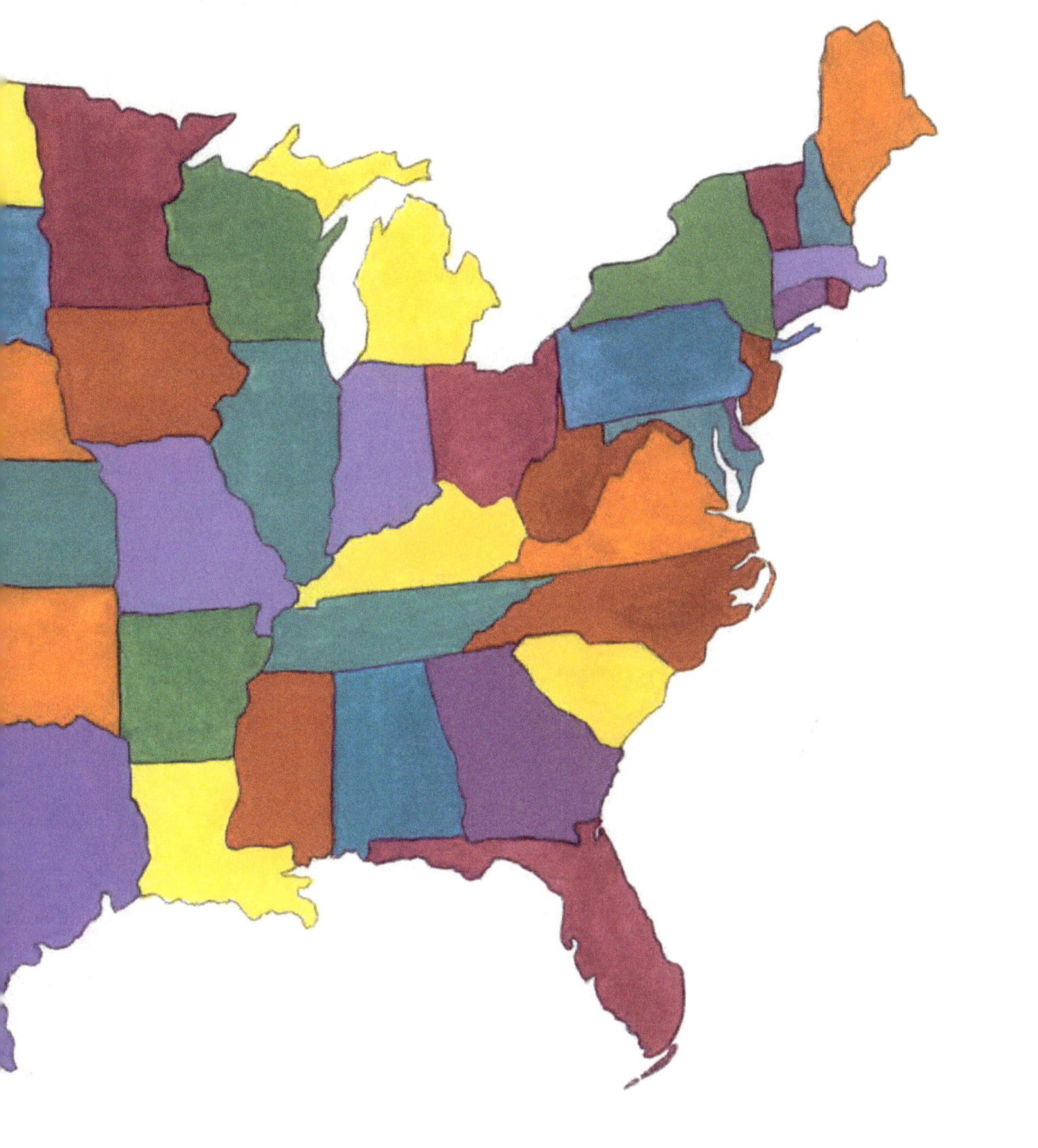

1.______________________________   5.______________________________

2.______________________________   6.______________________________

3.______________________________   7.______________________________

4.______________________________   8.______________________________

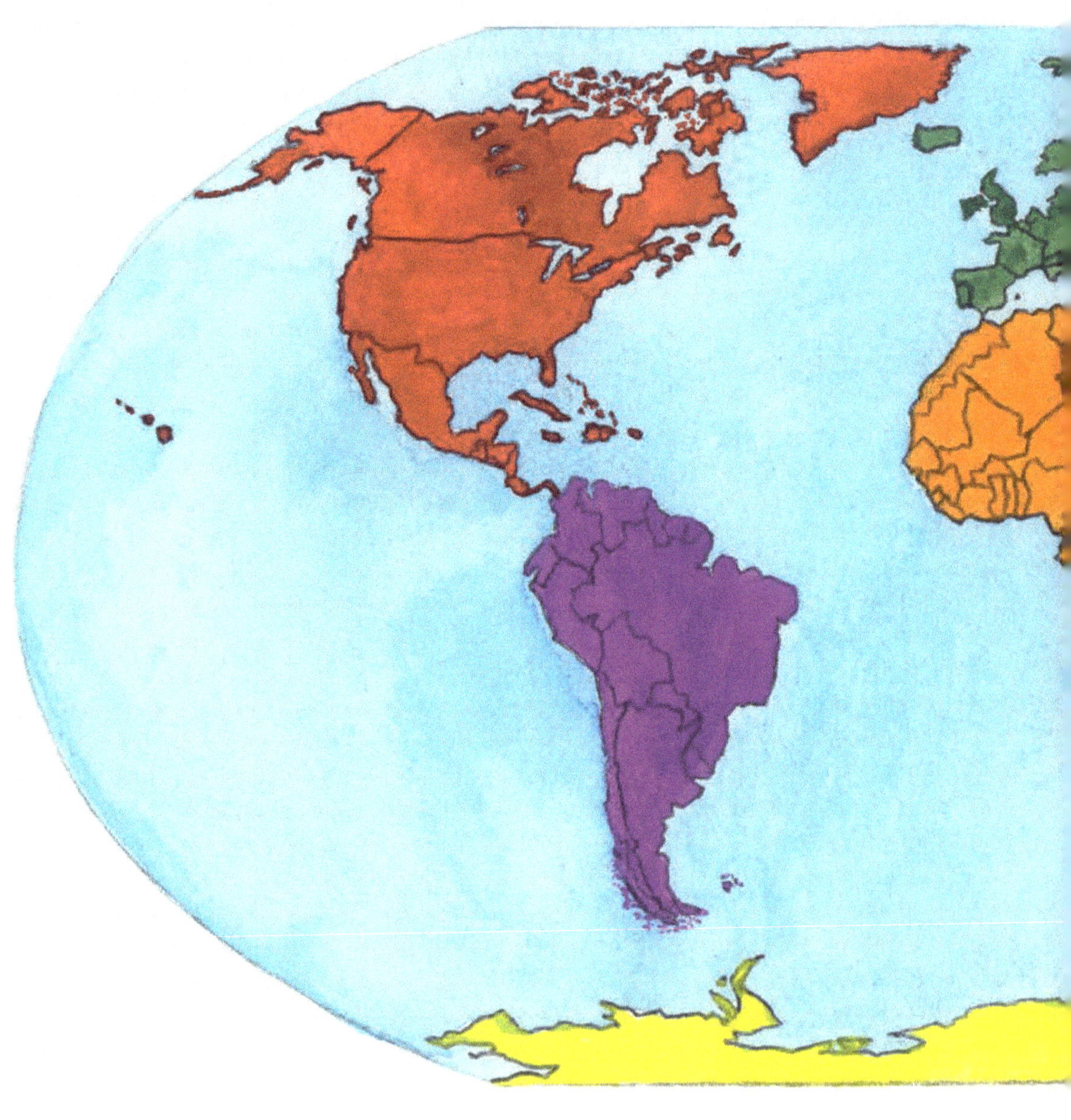

Here's a map of the world. Write down the places and bases where you've lived or visited and star them on your map:

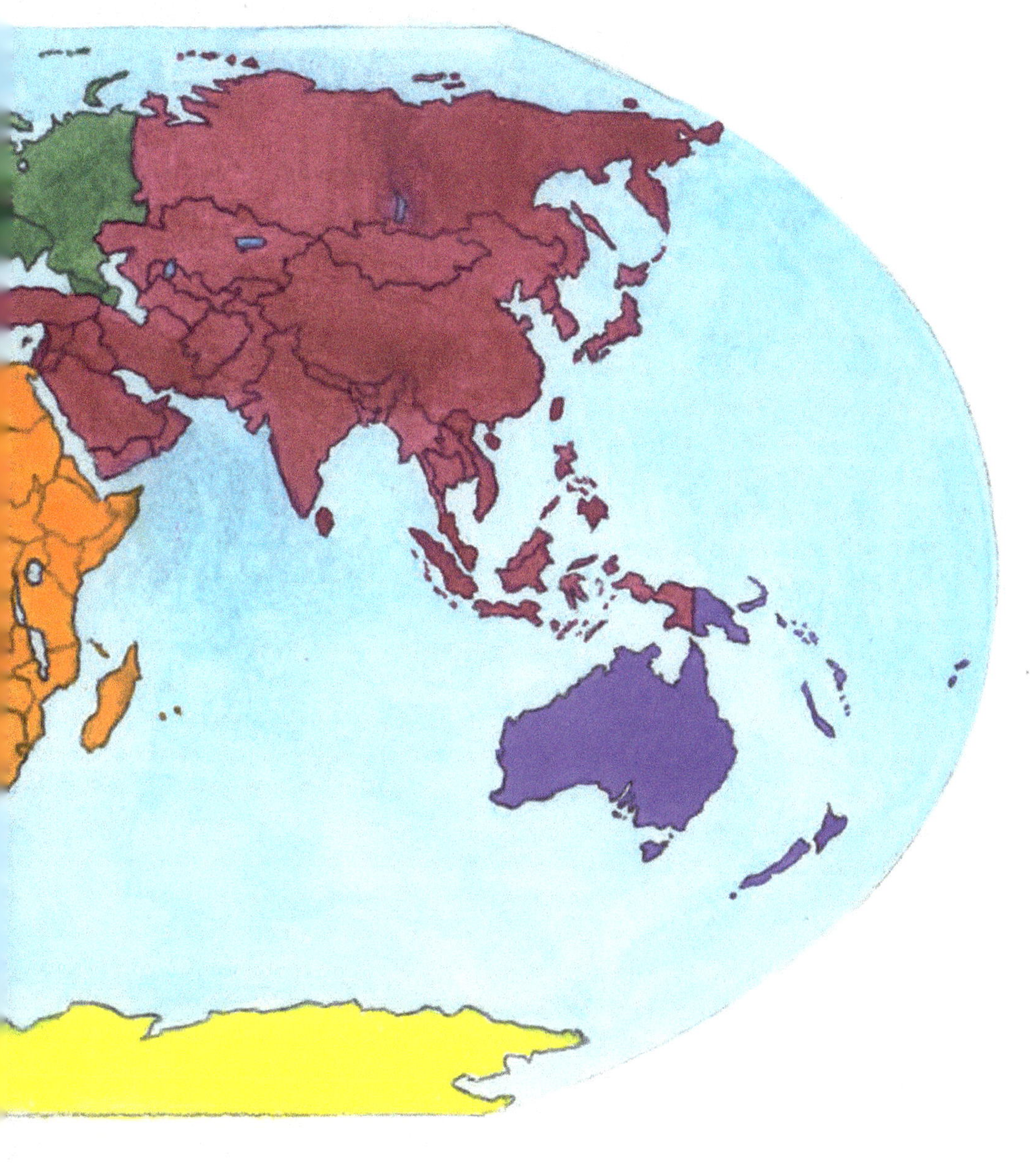

1.____________________   5.____________________

2.____________________   6.____________________

3.____________________   7.____________________

4.____________________   8.____________________

I know that moving can be hard for military kids. I used to not like moving because it meant that I had to pack up all my toys and leave my friends behind.

But now, I don't mind moving because I try to see it as an adventure with tons of new places to explore and awesome kids to meet!

Sometimes, I like to imagine that I am an explorer, like Lewis and Clark, and it's my mission to explore the new land! I take my mission very seriously and it helps me feel less sad and more excited about the cool things I get to discover!

What do you get excited about when you have to move? Draw or write about it in the frame.

What makes you sad when you have to move?
Draw or write about it in the frame.

Military kids get to live in really cool places, like Germany and Hawaii! I like to look back on all the places I've been and things I've done when I feel sad and want to remember happy times.

Create a timeline of
your military journey
on the next page.

MY MILITARY

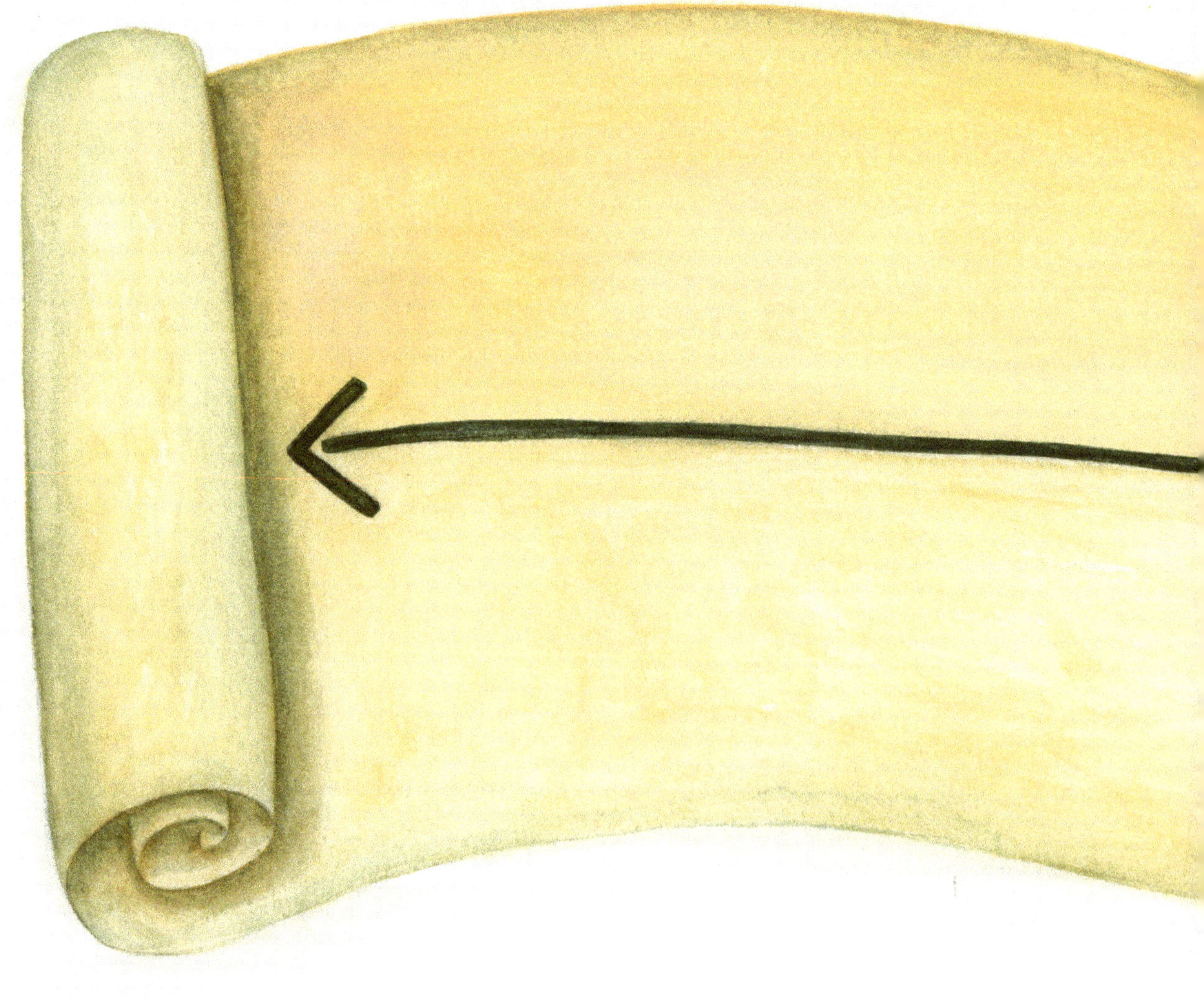

TIMELINE

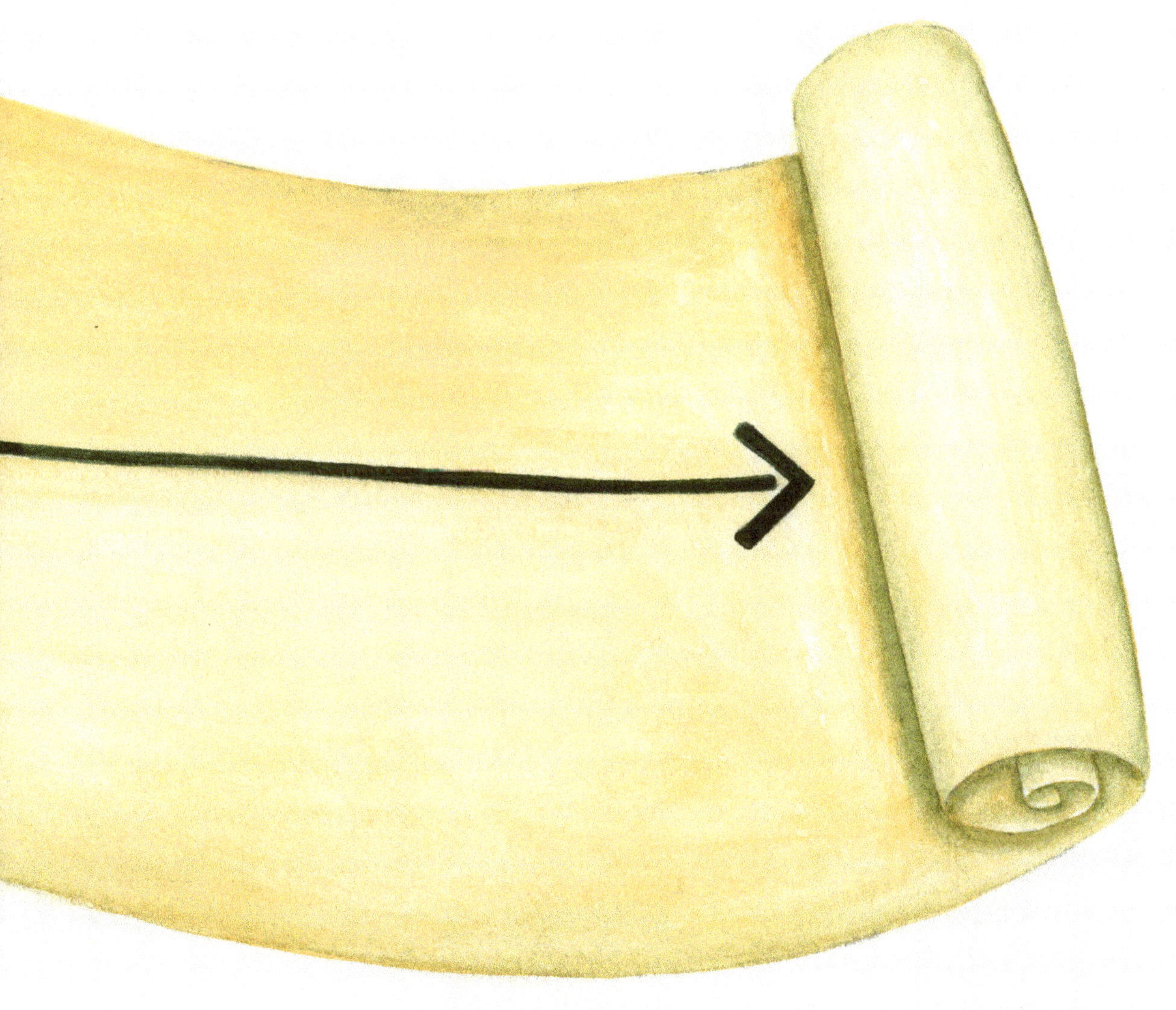

I've only been to 3 different schools, but I know other military kids who have been to lots and lots! Some kids have a hard time leaving their friends and teachers when they have to move, and that's okay.

Did you know that the average military kid changes schools 6 to 9 times? That's SO many different schools!

When we moved to North Carolina,
I was really sad. It took me a long time to feel
happy again. One trick I learned is called
"feel good statements," where I can
change my bad thoughts and find
something good to say to myself instead.

I miss my friends in Colorado. 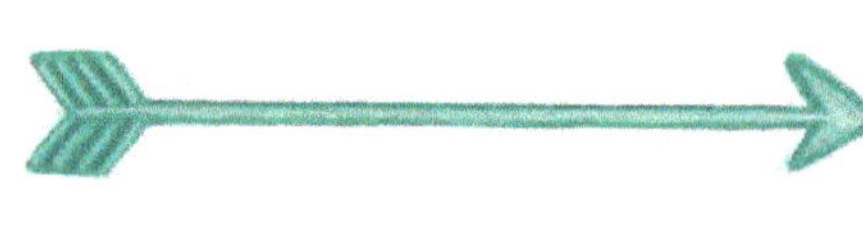 I can ask my mom or dad to call them or I can write them a letter.

I don't like my new school.  It takes some time to get used to a new place.

I miss my old house.  This house will start to feel like home. All of my toys are here and so is my family.

NOW YOU TRY

Before I was born, my dad fought bad guys, and he said it was one of the hardest things he ever had to do. After we moved to Fort Carson, my mom went away to fight bad guys for one year. It was really hard. Isabella and I were really sad when she left, and I know my dad was too. But before my mom left, we thought about different ways we could stay close to her.

I decided to keep a journal that I wrote in every day. When I would talk to mom on the phone or skype, I would read her my journal and tell her about everything that happened at home and at school. She kept a journal too, but she couldn't tell me everything that happened because it was "top secret." She said I didn't need to worry about bad guys because I had more important things to focus on...like homework!

MY JOURNAL

Write your own journal entry here.

Has your parent or guardian gone
away to fight bad guys, too?

____

____

What can you do to feel closer to
them when they are far away?

1. ____________________________

2. ____________________________

3. ____________________________

4. ____________________________

5. ____________________________

"Something I like to
do when Mommy goes away
is trace her hand and then trace my
hand in hers. Then Mommy writes 5 things
she loves about me in my hand, and I write
5 things I love about Mommy in her hand.
When I feel sad and miss
Mommy, I take our hands
out and hug them
close to my heart."

HERE, YOU CAN TRY THIS ACTIVITY TOO!

OUR HANDPRINTS

→

Even though being a military kid is difficult at times, I love it and wouldn't trade it for a million dollars! I get to travel all over the country, meet lots of super cool dudes and dudettes (like You!), and make tons of new and exciting memories!

What do you love about being a military kid?

1.____________________________________

2.____________________________________

3.____________________________________

Draw your favorite thing
about being a military kid.

I am proud to be a MILITARY KID!

Acknowledgments

I'd like to thank the people who have not only contributed
to the development of this book, but who have supported,
encouraged, loved, and given me wisdom along the way:
my parents and sisters; Derrick Numbers; Carolyn
Cordasco; my amazing illustrator; and my extended
military family. I'd also like to thank all of the military
kids out there who are truly extradorinary!

About the Author

MEGAN NUMBERS, MA, LPC is a former military spouse, grew up in a military family, and has 2 military kids of her own. She works as counselor for military children and families near Fort Bragg, NC. Her passion for working with military kids grew as she embarked on her dream of becoming a play therapist and earning her doctorate in counselor education and supervision. Megan quickly realized that military kids had limited resources that both illuminated the challenges they faced and provided concrete interventions to help them through military-related struggles. She saw a need for a resource and started developing this book that is loosely based on the stories of military kids she knows.

About the Illustrator

JAX BENNETT has always had a passion for both creating art and helping others. She's grateful to have made a career that has married the two together. After receiving her Bachelor of Fine Art in Illustration from the Rhode Island School of Design, Jax went on to earn her Master of Science in Art Therapy at Florida State University. As a Licensed Professional Counselor for the state of North Carolina and a Registered Play Therapist, Jax spends her days guiding and supporting children and teens through their therapeutic journeys. Jax also enjoys spending time with her family and friends, creating art, and going to the beach.

www.hellgatepress.com

CPSIA information can be obtained
at www.ICGtesting.com
Printed in the USA
LVHW07s1204250318
571043LV00007B/79/P